AF577197

ENGLISH CREAM

Sarah Lucas Michael Clark Don Brown Julian Simmons

SL
I thought I'll do three muses – or I was thinking of it like that, then I just thought well actually there doesn't need to be, there are all sorts of amounts of muses in history – and different ideas about how many there were in different places, not loads of different ideas ...but I can't remember who had what idea.
MC
I don't know about nine? – because I looked into it when I did that thing about Apollo for the Stravinsky Project.
SL
Three or nine are the ideas we're most familiar with, but somebody else thought there were ten. The other thing, that ten and that nine and that three, are not all the same bunch of muses, they're in different places – so in any case there's no absolute reason to stick to that number. There can be any amount of musing going on, can't there?
MC
Historically the female nude is something that men have always wanted – has always been a subject for men. For it to be a subject matter for a woman is a different thing. I mean for a man to walk into a room with nine naked women, is kind of like... a fantasy.
SL
Well that's another thing I've been thinking about for quite a long while... is you know having been so associated with feminist work, or that being in the mix as a subject – years ago – and I suppose I felt I had something to bring to it ...well it's not like I'm less of a feminist these days or something, but on the other hand I wouldn't know how to express it now. I've often wondered how do you bring that into work today. I didn't want to be an angry 'banging-on about something' person for the rest of my life, I didn't want that life for myself. Well then, how do you have that stuff in? In a way, just the fact that it is women – by women ...in that way I think it's a good way of having the feminist subject in, without having to be heavy-handed about it in any way – and with people standing for themselves, as real women.
MC
...and not idealised, it's actually how they really are.
SL
In some ways it's a macho job. Heavy. If you're doing something as big as half a body, that amount of plaster, water, plus the actual mould itself, you have to get on with it in a really robust way, it's not a namby-pamby sort of job or anything. It reminds me a bit of when you did, '*Oh My Goddess*' and the song '*Four Women*', it's that sort of notion in a way.
MC
I like the idea of the dynamic of women together. It's got a very different feeling than a group of men.
SL
Yes, maybe it would be interesting to do something with a group of men. The sculpture of me sitting on a table (*You Know What*, 1998) it was almost a frog-like position, that's what it looked like – or I did. There's one leg dangling off the table and the other leg up on top of the table like this, in plaster, with the actual vagina bit having a real cigarette, in it. Risking embarrassment or something – of me to do that myself at the time. Which was not dissimilar to Kris's pose here, but had one knee much more up. That was another really funny thing about it, I actually made it for a show I was doing in New York at Barbara's, years ago. I can't remember what I called the show, Supersensible, or maybe not? Anyway I liked it as a sculpture but I don't know if other people did. I remember standing there at the opening, being quite excited about this piece, I thought it was funny and confrontational – in a good way, but because the sculpture had it's back to where people came in, they'd see it from there first ...then I noticed people were sort of filing around the exhibition and as soon as they got around and saw what was going on with the cigarette, they'd just immediately look the other way and walk off in the opposite direction! I'm actually wondering what people will be thinking of it this time.
DB
They haven't got much choice, they'll turn away from one and then there's another one!
SL
When I was making that first one it was so much about the moment with the cigarette – than it is now. It's changed doing a lot more of them. But there's other funny things about them – being topless – because they're really topless!! I mean this whole notion of 'topless' it's a bit weird isn't it!? There's nothing topless about it! – having your tits out. It's 'top-out', or something. I like the cut off bit – that sense of the volume of somebody, which you don't ever see about yourself, the shapes it makes. For instance Margot makes a great heart shape.
JS
We were eating a lot of Mortadella. In Venetian delis it shouts out with its absolutely huge, pink man-made mass. Meat mush cast in a cylindrical mould and always with a terrazzo-mottled, precisely sliced flat section on view, like the cross-sections through the muses, yet a cartoon pink. I thought about this long and hard, a kind of unsavoury thought, like SPAM and Mortadella are – yet also sweet and pleasant, somehow like the future is – and how it's sectioned here and now.
SL
I definitely don't think they would be improved ...because that is a question I get asked... "why didn't you do the whole body?", but I don't think they'd be better sculptures for being the whole body, quite the opposite.
DB
No, clearly it's not necessary. When you look at this one, you don't think (certainly not from this view) that it's a topless figure. The whole thing is implied isn't it ...you've got the main bit.

SL

Yes exactly and it makes you look at them more I think, the fact it's not the whole, it's more intriguing ...otherwise there's things you take for granted about a whole figure.

DB

You'd look for something else if the whole figure was there – that might not necessarily be there anyway. It's not a bad question.

SL

I don't know if it would work just doing the top half. That would actually look like something terrible had happened.

DB

But also there's a tradition isn't there... of busts.

SL

Oh that's true actually though, yes, so there is a top half, it's busts!

DB

This is the opposite of a bust, it's the bottom. It's not a bad question is it? – "where are the tops", but then it leaves somehow. Like what would be here?... it could be elbows.

SL

Then you would absolutely have to include the head – and that puts in quite a different thing of what or who it's about or the facial expression, then inevitably the expression becomes the most important thing. Because in a way, putting the cigarettes in the bums or the vaginas turns that part of the body into a face ...they get their character that way. I don't think it's rude like if it was a real body. Also there's a bum cleavage sort of thing – and the way this has the bit of the bum cheeks at the front, in Kris in particular and Michele, that's a nice thing. Later on that first sculpture was in storage in Momart – and it went up in the fire. Recently I woke up one morning and thought let's remake that piece, but we'll do more of them. Then it occurred to me that it's a kind of muses theme. I mean it doesn't have to be, you don't have to see it as a muses theme but it kind of is a muses thing anyway whether you think of it like that or not. Even in the slight whimsicality of it – not that you can call muses whimsical, but you know what I mean, that kind of poetic slightly unearthly quality.

MC

Must be quite an unpleasant thing to put yourself through?

SL

It's not entirely pleasant and it's also devastatingly messy, not devastating, but quite messy really. Especially when things go wrong, which they always do. And because I work at home, this sounds ridiculous (and is maybe why people have studios) I don't always want to get into that kind of a mess. I get into it quite reluctantly in a way. Obviously you can get over that thing – about making a mess. This time we did it with one person posing and two people putting on the bandages. Even then it takes a good hour, sometimes more, that's a long time for someone to stay in one position. It's hard work for all concerned.

JS

My studio-office table, that Sarah's had from the year dot, oak with a brown linoleum top, is the one Sarah cast Michele on. Often our household furniture gets incorporated into sculptures, they're handy, obviously look good and have wear. When it's a table that's working well, it's always a wrench – for me. I like a large table, Sarah's not that keen as they get in the way of dance-floor space. Anyway this one stayed, along with an imprint of Michele's bum – a large B where the lino is slightly cracked and inhabited with a peppery black mold. I see this perplexing organism every day. Like the Mortadella... and blue cheese, it's conspiratorially seductive.

SL

Actually when you've done that bit and think "oh great that's the hard work over", the actual filling up of the moulds are worse ...and more hard work.

MC

Really?

SL

It's quite a tricky business as it's a whole one-piece thing. It's not the way you'd do it if you were going to do it really properly, but that'd be another job that I would really hate. I love doing it the rough way. A lot of things go wrong, leaks.

MC

Is it hard to get the seam on the leg, is that a choice you make?

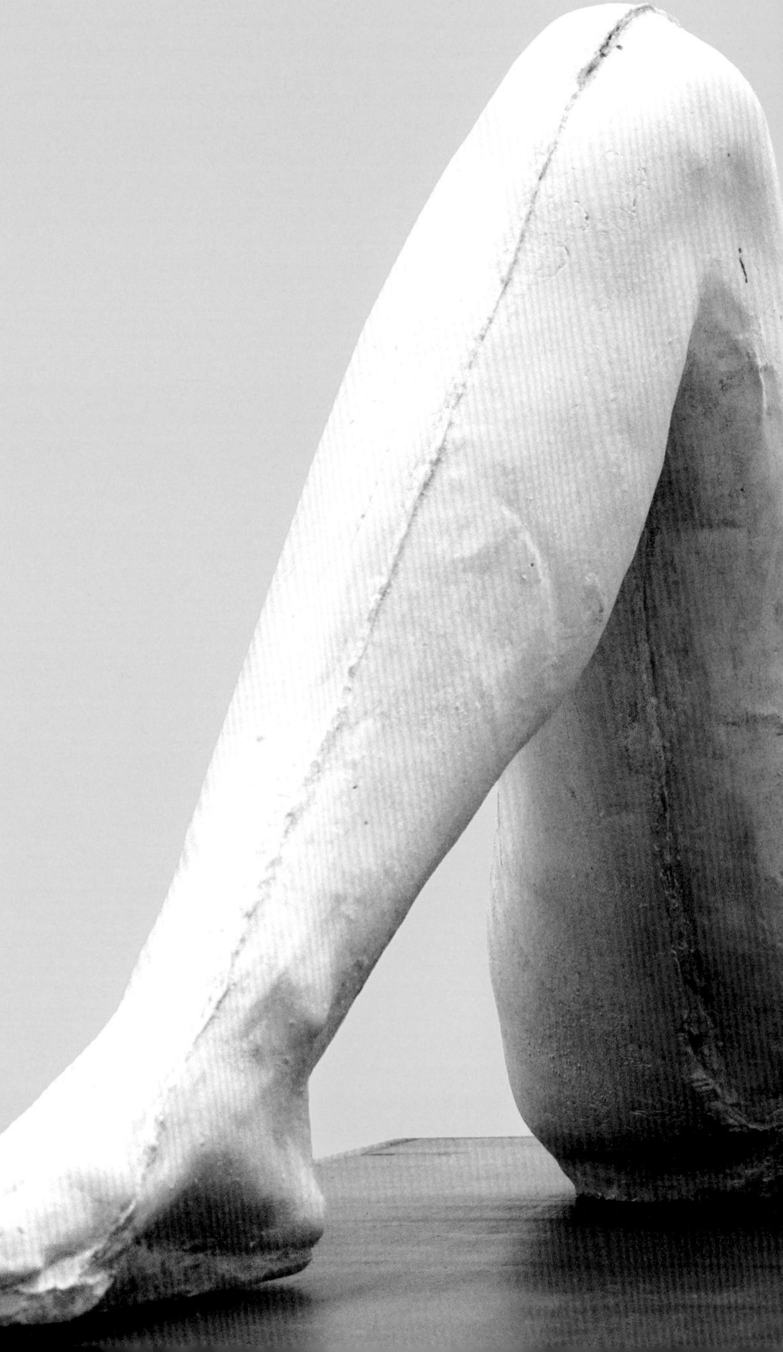

SL
It's a choice you make but some of those bits you change as you're actually doing it, as you suddenly realise …you know you have to think on your feet – that's part of it. No actually, if you've got the right gang of people it's really enjoyable …and the fact it's obviously a bit intimate and stuff, is also nice! So in fact it's being made by women, certain women, who as well as being the makers they are also the muses! Although that won't be the case with the next lot, but they're all brilliant friends of mine. It's all those elements that alleviate it from being just a job of work. As a job of work it'd be a horrible job, but in the right circumstances and camaraderie it's a really enjoyable job. It was special all of the muses coming individually… it brings you close together, even with friends that you're very close to anyway. All being women it's gentle but also has to be quite fast, robust, no messing about.
None of them are as simple as they look either, we tried to get things a bit asymmetrical. So that's who we all are, people very close to me, people I'm actually involved with in practical ways in my life, which I think is also part of the ethos of the show – and I tend to be a bit like that anyway… like to do things with people, like to live like that.
DB
You described them as 'muses' to Yoko; she said "all the muses are meeting".
SL
All the muses are meeting! – it's a nice thing …we've become muses now! I think the cigarette gesture really suits musing, because you do muse when you're having a cigarette in way don't you? and there's something quite insouciant about it …also it's a bit of titillation isn't it?!
DB
Well it's a long time since I smoked, though I know it's that time-off thing – from the world, where you just sit there, for a little while.
JS
You can play a flute.
SL
With your bum?
JS
…oh no, with your vagina.
SL
Oh.
MC
Someone told me the vagina inhales before orgasm.
JS
When you just squat up and down it inhales.
MC
Arh, no, it was the penis, sorry; he said he got more women that way.
JS
What do you think, if there is one, a theme of the show?
SL
erm
…custard!!!
MC
What do they call that in French, it's something Anglaise?
SL
Creme Anglaise.
JS
English Cream!
SL
Themes are tricky aren't they, women is one of the themes, it's for women …and it is women. I'd like it to give rise to the sensation that the things do make some kind of sense, not exactly sense necessarily, but they're very particularly related to each other in a plausible sort of way, not overly plausible, but you don't question that. In terms of the operative principle I like the idea that it's floating islands – in custard.
MC
Like Venice.
SL
Yes a bit like Venice!

JS
Takes me back several centuries to the so called Floating World – of Japan, a place seething with white-painted women where your dreams could be bought …hedonistic pleasures, for a while.
SL
Colour is really tricky, I mean I like the idea that the whole thing looks like a painting, like to be in it, is to be in a painting.
JS
You know how paint colour charts give colours names, to make them more appealing I suppose, well the colour we choose for the walls behind the sculptures was aptly named Banana Dream 3.
MC
You were saying about walking into a painting and the table being the whole world …because I think of your things being the thing itself – is the whole thing, you know what I mean?
SL
Yes exactly, so when you go into an exhibition, it's not that I make narrative work or I want it to be narrative, but there is a sense in which there's a story, or the sculptures or whatever it might be, are a cast of characters. You're putting a bunch of characters in a room and hoping they're having a party or something.
MC
I love the idea of walking into a painting.
SL
So you can walk into an exhibition, anybody's, and you might come out feeling like it was a bit of a waste of time, or you actually had some sort of a good time. Obviously the aim is people come out thinking "yeah! I got some satisfaction out of that". Which I suppose you think about when you are doing a show?…
MC
Yes, smells coming through the air-conditioning – encapsulating all the senses.
SL
That's a nice idea.
MC
Not rotten eggs.
JS
What's the significance of yellow?
SL
I suppose it's an eggy sort of thing yellow, comes back to eggs. Which I've always had in the mix somehow …and then thinking about the whiteness of the plaster sculptures – the muses, it suddenly occurred to me to think about them as floating islands, *îles flottantes* – the dessert. So custard became relevant and then I thought custard is good, because it's basically eggs. The muses are the meringues and the yellow on the walls is the custard… and actually the caramel is the varnished wooden furniture. I've always had a thing about eggs and eggnog and custard and stuff and actually I've had a thing about yellow. When I first ever had a room of my own, I must have been 14 or 15, I painted it white and put a yellow stripe 'round it.
MC
The significance of eggs…?
SL
That thing that people will (or I thought being a sort of born cynic) – that people will think they'll make a painting of an egg and it'll mean something, that got on my tits.
MC
So it's got a resonance but it doesn't necessarily…
SL
…but actually it's empty, it's just a fucking painting of an egg!
MC
I know a woman who calls her kids 'my fried eggs', which is quite unusual, never heard that before.
SL
It was actually a kind of a way of saying your tits are too small.

SL
Margot and Margot's bum.
DB
On a freezer.
SL
That's not because she's a chef, although it's quite a funny thing like that.
JS
Yes they're all a bit like that. There's Sadie riding the waves – like Britannia on the back of a big old penny – which suits. Sarah, two sculptures, both ways in which you like getting to know people …having a chat down the pub and reading. Also more formally, there's Michele on the manager's desk forming a great M …and Yoko making a Y at her crutch.
SL
I mean she is very Earth-mother-ish, Margot. For me using the freezer – apart from just the white thing, which I thought would be nice – the different white surfaces, it really is a landscape format, in a way that whole piece is – and I think Margot is somehow. The other one in here – which is me on the bar stool, it was just an instinctive thing to put it in that corner, actually I thought at the time it reminded me of that Martin Kippenberger piece where he wears the dunce's hat and stands in the corner. I thought afterwards Margot being so motherish and me being in the corner on the bar stool, actually does say something about my relationship with my own mum – which was a bit weird at times. Well I think… not that Margot is anything like my mum …well I won't go into any more detail than that. Because you know you set up an exhibition and then you can… …you've got all the things you think you are doing, but actually then you can look at yourself. You don't think you're making an autobiography but to a great extent you are, even in that Freudian-slip way – that you don't realise what you are revealing about yourself, as you're not thinking about it from that angle, your purpose is something else.
DB
Well in that sense, it's impossible for things not to have meaning. That's the whole worry about making art, generally about what is it. I can remember thinking I won't think of it like that any more, I'll just make some stuff. Then it occurred to me a few years later that it doesn't matter anyway because it's bound to be meaningful in some way, autobiographical or whatever, have some sort of significance.
SL
Yes I used to worry about that a lot.
DB
I mean even just choosing that freezer – the idea that it's so sealed…
SL
And cold.
DB
Impenetrable to some extent.
SL
…that's the thing you see, because my mum when I was – and I think all my brothers and sisters think this – when we were little kids anyway, she wasn't entirely …this is too much to say really… but there was something about her that was a little bit cold, she wasn't a very huggy sort of person.
DB
But it's also like a fridge-freezer is owning a bit of another world, there's another landscape in there …it's an alien environment inside.
SL
Yes and even on the outside it is, isn't it? – a bit of an alien environment.
JS
A white god.
SL
That's the other thing about having the show coloured yellow…
DB
Unifies the whole thing, rather than just a collection of objects.
SL
Yeah but because it's a colour you look at the objects more in a painterly way – of what their colours are doing, you think about it more, or I do, than if it's in a white room, where I think you'd just focus on them as objects. Floating islands are the order of the day! – Britain is a floating island, Venice is various floating islands, so is Britain I suppose.
JS
Maybe also women?
SL
Maybe…

WOMEN ARE FLOATING ISLANDS

14 prints, each in an edition of 12 + 3 AP's
Editions 1 - 4 inclusive, sold as portfolio sets
Editions 5 - 12 available individually
104.3 x 78 cm / 41 x 30 3/4 in

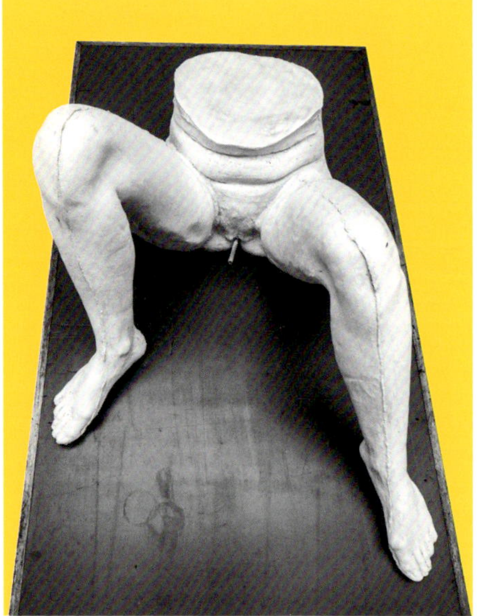

SADIE LOOKING LIKE BRITANNIA
CONFRONTATIONAL MICHELE MAKING A FACE (HIGH)
CONFRONTATIONAL MICHELE MAKING A FACE (LEVEL)

MY BUM ON THE BAR-STOOL
ME AGAIN – READING POETRY
'EDIT' ACTUALLY AS SHE'S ESTONIAN

KRIS SAYING HELLO TO THE BOYS

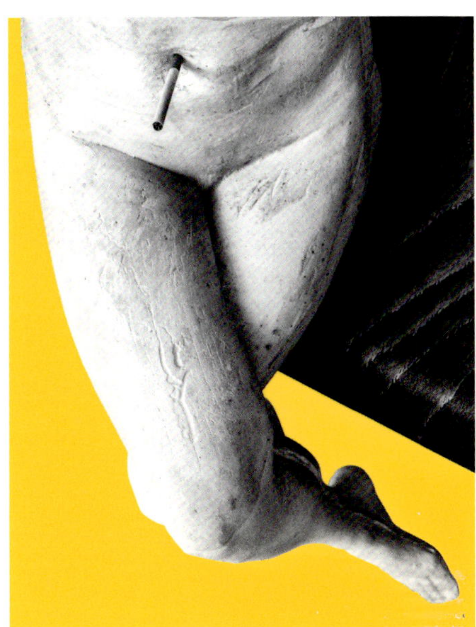

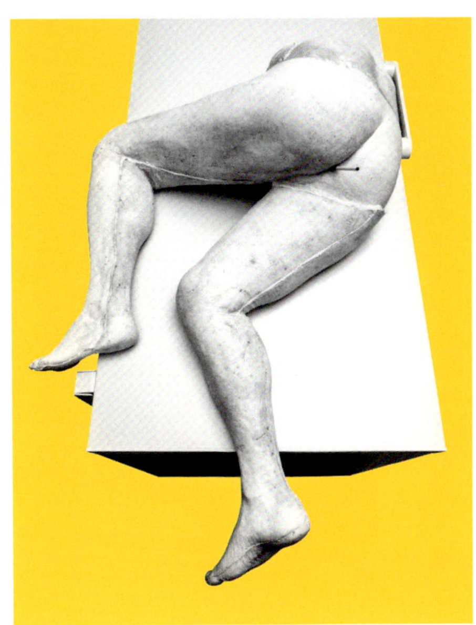

A VERY STATELY PAULINE
YOKO SMOKING THROUGH HER BELLY-BUTTON EYE (LOW)
YOKO SMOKING THROUGH HER BELLY-BUTTON EYE (HIGH)

MARGOT IN LANDSCAPE FORMAT MOTHER-EARTH LIKE (LEVEL)
MARGOT IN LANDSCAPE FORMAT MOTHER-EARTH LIKE (HIGH)
PATRICIA THE SORB-APPLE (LOW)

PATRICIA THE SORB-APPLE (CLOSE)

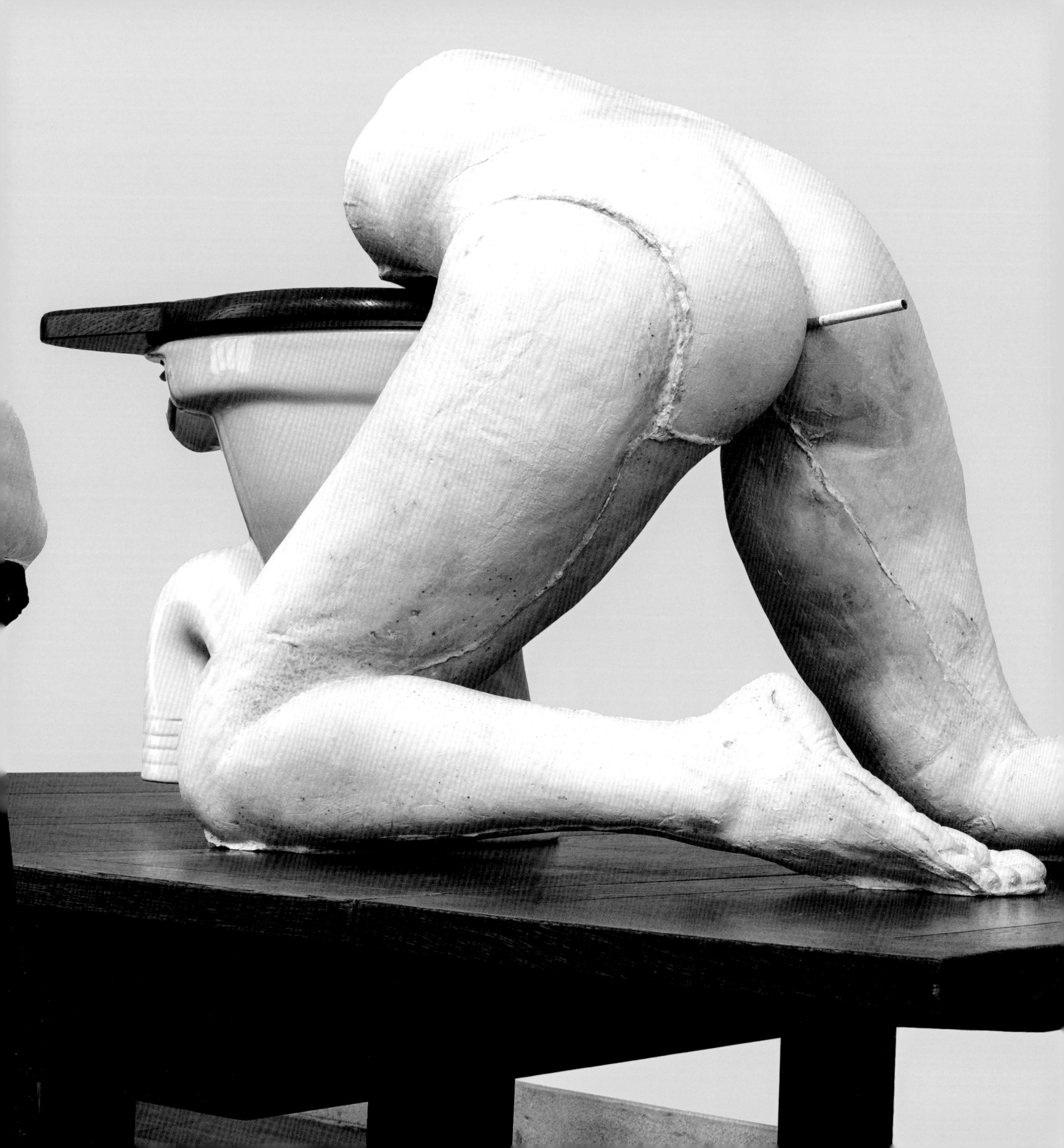

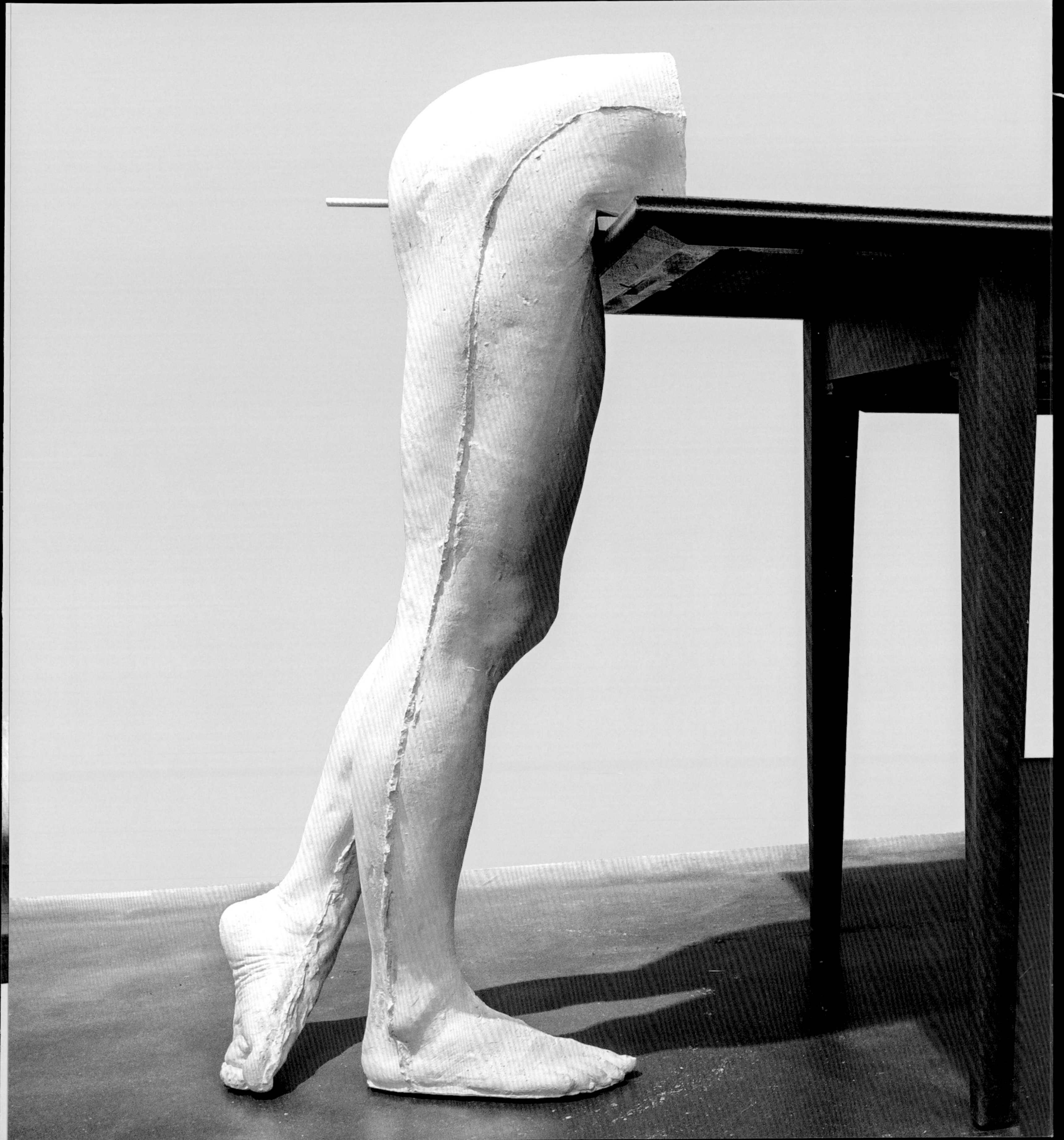

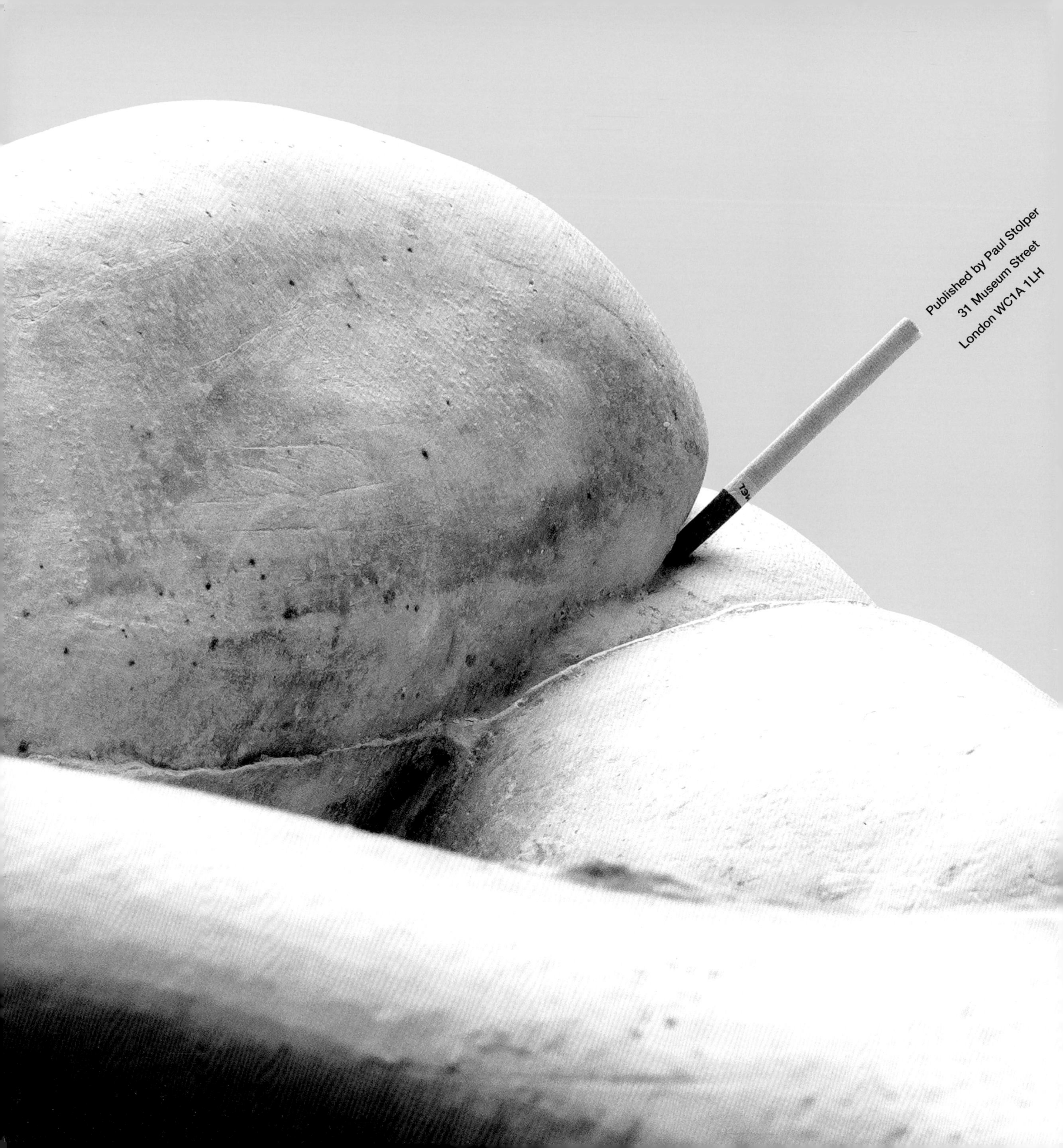

Published by Paul Stolper
31 Museum Street
London WC1A 1LH